A Spiritual Exercise
for the Grieving

ELWYN A. SMITH

Fortress Press   Philadelphia

COPYRIGHT © 1984 BY FORTRESS PRESS

Library of Congress Cataloging in Publication Data

Smith, Elwyn A. (Elwyn Allen), 1919-
   A spiritual exercise for the grieving.

   1. Consolation – Prayer books and devotions – English. 2. Bereavement – Religious aspects – Christianity – Prayerbooks and devotions. I. Title.
BV4905.2.S58 1984   242′.4   84-47935
ISBN 0-8006-1807-6 (pbk.)

K981C84   Printed in the United States of America   1-1807

IN MEMORIAM
Justin Patrick Gerlach
October 10-13, 1982

Contents

Contents

A Spiritual Exercise

Spiritual exercise strengthens the soul just as physical exercise strengthens the body. Times of pain and grief offer special opportunities for the development of spiritual life — but not without effort and discipline. Grieving is a process that seeks completion — yet we can become mired in our emotion and not move forward. If we are to grow through grief, spiritual exercise is needed. This little book of prayer and reflection is intended for that purpose.

Any good system of exercise is progressive. This book opens with themes that occupy most people who are grieving and proceeds through a series of steps designed to develop the soul and mind. Themes change as your experience moves forward. Each deals with both God and your feelings, bringing these together. Every person's experience is unique, so if you find that a theme proposed for one day helps you on another, change the order to suit your need.

How to Use This Book of Prayer and Reflection

This book provides guidance for three periods of prayer, reflection, and praise each day for seven days. It is designed primarily for the grieving but may be used by persons experiencing many kinds of trouble. Its themes are chosen to deal with the universal questions that arise in times of stress and to bring to the reader the wealth of understanding and comfort provided by the Bible. The materials may be used many times over, since the meaning of fundamental themes of Christian faith is disclosed at ever-deeper levels as we grow in Christ.

Morning: Each day has its theme, memory verse, and Scripture readings. Morning is a time for prayer and thinking about the day's verse. Prayers and verses may be read aloud. The morning exercise concludes with a blessing.

Noon: The Prayer for the Hour may be used to bless the food. After the meal, read the Scriptures and the Reflection on the Theme. Your time of grief should give you a broader grasp of important themes of the Bible and a store of newly memorized portions of Scripture that can sustain you the rest of your life.

Evening: This portion is to be used just before you retire. The Prayer for the Night speaks of feelings many people have — you may add your own personal prayer. The Theme for Meditation is intended to focus your thoughts. How easy it is to lie awake worrying. How tempting is self-pity. But these do not help us toward healing. Let the theme take possession of your mind and give you peace. Trust God for all that you cannot do. Repeat the theme verse and the memory verse to yourself. Murmur them, say them aloud — use them in any manner that lets them carry your mind, like an offering, to the Lord.

DAY ONE
Meaning

MORNING

Dedication of the Day

Dear Lord, I come to you now to offer this day's thoughts to you. I would begin by dedicating my mind to your glory. I ask for a special gift: give me some sense of the meaning of my grief. I pray in the name of Jesus Christ your Son. Amen.

Adoration

Thou, Lord, didst found the earth in the beginning,
and the heavens are the work of thy hands;
they will perish, but thou remainest;
they will all grow old like a garment,
like a mantle thou wilt roll them up,
and they will be changed.
But thou art the same,
and thy years will never end.
    (Heb. 1:10–12; quoted from Ps. 102:25–27)

A Word to Memorize

Thy will be done, on earth as it is in heaven.

(Matt. 6:10)

There is perhaps no other phrase more often on the lips of Christians than this petition from the Lord's Prayer. It has a special purpose in today's spiritual exercise: it is our prayer for understanding.

All persons instinctively assume that life and events have meaning. It is very disturbing when deep grief causes us to doubt the meaningfulness of life. Our minds are flooded with questions: Why did this happen to me? How can I go on? Questions, but few answers. We may not even know what to pray for.

Many a philosopher has exhausted both imagination and intellect searching for the source of meaning. With a single phrase Jesus puts the correct petition into our mouths: "Thy will be done, on earth as it is in heaven."

The Blessing

If we have died with him, we shall also live with him;

if we endure, we shall also reign with him;

if we deny him, he also will deny us;

if we are faithless, he remains faithful —

for he cannot deny himself.

(2 Tim. 2:11–13)

NOON

A Prayer for the Hour

Dear Father, I am grateful for your gifts of strength in both body and soul. I want to grow into the full maturity that you intend for me, and I ask you to bless the grief I am now experiencing. Give me a life that is rich with meaning. Show me your will in the Name of Jesus our Lord. Amen.

The Scriptures

Ps. 69:1-18. The poet's cry for God's help in great distress.

Hebrews 11. How God gave meaning to the lives of the great figures of the Old Testament.

A Reflection on the Meaning-filled Life

Those who grieve often feel that life has lost meaning. During periods of physical weakness, often burdened by great expense, a grieving person with many years of useful life ahead may fall into despair.

People do not usually ask questions about life's meaning until they are jolted, perhaps by a death in the family. In ordinary experience, meaning and purpose are obvious and do not require much thought. There is nothing mysterious about why we install storm windows in the fall—it saves money — or why we put on the screens in the spring. The larger reason beyond the simple answer, "To keep the flies out," goes no farther than personal comfort and protection of health.

We may know very well the short-range explanation of a death in the family. Often with painful feelings of guilt we reflect on what we might have done differently. But beyond that — what? What useful purpose can be served by the death of a young parent or of a newborn child? What is the meaning of such events for the lives of those who must go on?

We realize how fragile our general sense of life's meaning really is. Work that was once exciting now seems futile; the daily regime of rearing children loses its joy; everything seems empty. Withdrawal and depression are often brought on by grief.

Today's Scripture meets us at this low point in our lives. How did all these biblical people survive? By faith, replies the author of The Letter to the Hebrews: faith in the goodness and guidance of God. Abraham had no "career objective" when he left his people "to go out to a place which he was to receive as an inheritance." He knew nothing of what lay ahead. He simply trusted God — and as his life unfolded, its meaning became apparent.

Even in the very last hour of life we may have difficulty saying exactly what our life means. But meaning is not lacking simply because we do not discern it. "These all died in faith, not having received what was promised," the author of Hebrews wrote concerning these ancients — but they *did* believe there was direction and purpose to their existence. They spent their lives "seeking a homeland," having lived every hour by faith, not by sight.

Much of what we think we "see" is illusory. Meaning is a gift of God. To be open to his good-will is the secret of the meaning-filled life.

My Prayer for This Day

Dear Father in heaven, I confess that there are times when I do not understand why things are as they are. Yet I do believe that you are supreme; I believe that your vision of me is more real than my own. Give me faith to see myself as you see me. If my vision is sometimes confused, let me trust that you are leading me to your own house. Through Jesus I pray. Amen.

The Blessing

Now may the God of peace who brought again from the dead our Lord Jesus, the great shepherd of the sheep, by the blood of the eternal covenant, equip you with everything good that you may do his will, working in you that which is pleasing in his sight, through Jesus Christ; to whom be glory for ever and ever. Amen.

(Heb. 13:20–21)

EVENING

A Prayer for the Night

Our Father, who art in heaven, hallowed be thy name, thy kingdom come, thy will be done, on earth as it is in heaven. Give us this day our daily bread, and forgive us our trespasses, as we forgive those who trespass against us, and lead us not into temptation, but deliver us from evil. For thine is the kingdom, and the power, and the glory, for ever and ever. Amen.

A Theme for Meditation

Hallowed be thy name.

(Matt. 6:9)

"Hallowed" simply means to be made holy. "Let thy name be made holy," we say in the Lord's Prayer. The worshiper ponders a single thought about God, concentrates on it, and keeps other concerns at a distance. Tonight, ponder the memorized verse: "Thy will be done, on earth as it is in heaven." Repeat it to yourself in shortened form: "Thy will be done." To pray thus is to make God's name holy. You are confessing that he is the source of your meaning.

DAY TWO
Separation

MORNING

Dedication of the Day

Heavenly Father, the mornings are the worst for
me. The night leaves me defenseless and the pain of
what has happened overwhelms me. The one I love
has been taken away and I cannot bear it.
Sometimes I feel separated even from you. Help me
to know how to respond to my feelings and to the
people who come to comfort me. I thank you for
them; I see you coming to me through their love.
Please help me to cope with this grief. For Jesus'
sake. Amen.

Adoration

O depth of wealth, wisdom, and knowledge in
God! How unsearchable his judgements, how un-
traceable his ways! Who knows the mind of the
Lord? Who has been his counsellor? Who has ever

19

made a gift to him, to receive a gift in return?
Source, Guide, and Goal of all that is — to him be
glory for ever! Amen.

(Rom. 11:33–36, NEB)

A Word to Memorize

There is . . . nothing in all creation that can
separate us from the love of God in Christ Jesus our
Lord.

(Rom. 8:38–39, NEB)

Separation from persons we love and who have
loved us is perhaps the most painful experience
possible. Many separations strip us of needed sup-
port. Worst of all is the feeling of separation from
God. If God seems to wear the face of a judge or to
have turned away from us, what is left for us? To
St. Paul's list of powers that separate us we could
add some of our own: guilt feelings, remorse,
anger. In the face of such alienating emotion St.
Paul declares in words that Christians have
remembered for centuries: "Nothing in all creation . . . can separate us from the love of God in
Christ Jesus our Lord."

The Blessing

Come, let us return to the Lord;
for he has torn us and will heal us,
    he has struck us and he will bind up our
      wounds. . . .

Let us humble ourselves, let us strive to know the
    Lord,
    whose justice dawns like morning light,
    and its dawning is as sure as the sunrise.

(Hos. 6:1-3, NEB)

NOON

A Prayer for the Hour

Dear heavenly Father, I thank you for the Word
you have spoken to me and I ask you to help me
understand it. I thank you for giving me the will to
pray, even when I do not feel like it. Grant me a
strong sense of your presence, even when life seems
most desolate to me; and give me the clarity of
mind I need to survive. In the Name of Jesus your
Son. Amen.

The Scriptures

Lam. 1:12–16. The grief of the prophet at the plight
    of Israel.
Rom. 8:26–39. How God responds to our distress.

A Reflection on Separation

The word "separation" often triggers painful
memories. We may remember our first separation
from our parents, the first day at school, or the
first trip to summer camp. Adulthood brings its
own kinds of suffering: the pain of widowhood lies

in the sudden, utterly shocking separation from a beloved spouse. Separation stands at the center of a whole circle of pain: loneliness, alienation, anxiety, despair.

For what do we grieve? For the loss of our intimate bond with the beloved; for the end of active loving. A couple anticipating the birth of their child experiences a steady building up of the powerful inward resolution and commitment that prepares them for parenthood — and then the baby dies. That is a very special agony, made all the more painful by frustration, disorientation, and the mother's physical condition.

The psalms and the prophets often speak of God's pain at his rejection by his own people, and Christians see in the event of the cross the climax of God's agony. St. Paul says to the Romans: God "did not spare his own Son, but gave him up for us all; and with this gift how can he fail to lavish upon us all he has to give?" (Rom. 8:32, NEB.) God's acceptance of his separation from his beloved Son becomes the very basis of hope.

In the same breath, St. Paul speaks of the life beyond separation. Christ, "who died, and, more than that, was raised from the dead," has returned to his Father. The grief that afflicted God at the death of his Son is overcome by resurrection and Christ is seen as the first of many, an "earnest" — that is, a trustworthy promise — of things to come.

Because of the cross, the power of separation, loneliness, alienation, and despair to convince us that life really is meaningless is broken. Even while we grieve we can know God's loving achievement. "Nothing in death or life, in the realm of spirits or superhuman powers, . . . in the forces of the universe . . . nothing in all creation . . . can separate us from the love of God in Christ Jesus our Lord." Our numbed feelings may leave us isolated from that divine love for a time, but our Father patiently awaits the reawakening of our faith.

My Prayer for This Day

Blessed Father, I have heard your promise to help me and I ask you for the special gifts I need to survive this time of pain. You must be my sufficiency, for I feel very inadequate. I do not yet see what you are doing in my life. Teach me to live patiently with this blindness to you. Let my very ignorance become an occasion for a new step of trust. Resolve my grief according to your will. In Jesus' Name I pray. Amen.

The Blessing

O Lord, my soul shall live with thee;
   do thou give my spirit rest.
   Restore me and give me life.

                              (Isa. 38:16, NEB)

EVENING

A Prayer for the Night

Lord Jesus, in the night my grief comes back, pouring over me, and I cannot help myself. I ask you now to send your Spirit into my mind and heart and affirm your love for me. Let me not awaken to tears but to thoughts of your care; and if I weep, let my tears draw me closer to all who grieved for you when you were taken from them. Lord, let the return of the morning be a sign to me of your rising. Give me hope in the restoration of the whole world when there will be no more death, no more separation, and no more tears. In Jesus' Name. Amen.

A Theme for Meditation

> In everything . . . he co-operates for good with those who love God and are called according to his purpose.
>
> (Rom. 8:28, NEB)

Most of us are familiar with this verse in the King James translation: "All things work together for good to them that love God, to them who are the called according to his purpose." This is very hard for a grieving person to believe. Some things seem so completely bad. This verse does not say that bad is good; it says that God's power and the mystery of his will are actively at work to wring good consequences from truly evil events.

Tonight let us wait for God's grace to surprise us. Can the consequences of grief actually be good? "Wait on the Lord. . . . Wait, I say, on the Lord."

DAY THREE
Tears

MORNING

Dedication of the Day

Blessed Father, you have given me another day of life. Once I took my days for granted, but no longer. This day is like a vase waiting to be filled—perhaps with beauty, perhaps with tears. Whatever it may hold, help me to pray and to hear your Word. Through Jesus my Savior. Amen.

Adoration

Give unto the Lord the glory due unto his name;
Worship the Lord in the beauty of holiness. . . .
The Lord will give strength unto his people;
The Lord will bless his people with peace.

(Ps. 29:2, 11, KJV)

A Word to Memorize

Behold, the dwelling of God is with men. . . . He

will wipe away every tear from their eyes, and death shall be no more.

(Rev. 21:3–4)

John of Patmos was writing to Christians who lived under great stress. Many expected to be executed because of the refusal of believers to make sacrifices to the Roman emperor. Loved ones had been killed and the world seemed about to give way to God's new age.

John speaks to the tears of the people of God. Further suffering lay ahead, but death would never conquer life. Even while the Christian people wept, they were reminded that God was the master of grief and death.

The Christian does not live solely for the present. The sorrows we experience today will never be forgotten, but our pain is part of a larger life whose end is joy. By faith, Christians can see God's own kingdom from afar and rejoice.

"Behold, the dwelling of God is with men. . . . He will wipe away every tear from their eyes, and death shall be no more."

The Blessing

Arise, shine; for your light has come,
    and the glory of the Lord has risen upon you.
For behold, darkness shall cover the earth,
    and thick darkness the peoples;

but the Lord will arise upon you,
    and his glory will be seen upon you.

(Isa. 60:1–2)

NOON

A Prayer for the Hour

O Lord, this is your holy place. You have made the day and the night, great prairies and tiny dens, even this room. Give me your blessing for this hour and help me hear your Word. Bless all who pray for me. In the Savior's Name. Amen.

The Scriptures

Isa. 30:19–26. The Lord's answer to those who weep.

Luke 13:34–35. Jesus lamenting the refusal of his people.

A Reflection on Tears

The very first thing a newborn baby does is to cry. And as life draws to a close, there are tears. In between are tears of anger, sympathy, frustration, and grief.

There is more to our tears than the immediate pressures that cause them. As people grow older or as health deteriorates, the conviction grows that grief lies at the heart of life. Does not every good thing end in sadness? Happy marriages are ended by the death of a partner. We get well only to fall sick again. So beyond all immediate causes of tears we are crying for life itself. We feel keenly the grievousness that lies at its very heart.

Jesus shed tears more than once but never more significantly than when he wept for the stubborn refusal of Jerusalem to receive the Messiah. His grief and the grief of all humankind came to a climax at the cross. There God himself grieved because of our refusal.

But the cross and its tears were followed by Jesus' resurrection. The women who found the tomb empty wept for joy. Those were very different tears.

When we are weeping in grief, we can remember that the time was to come when the tears of Jesus' friends would be signs of joy. We ordinarily assume that life is followed by death — is that not the order we see everywhere? But the raising of Lazarus, Jairus' daughter, and Jesus has another message: death is followed by life, defeat by victory.

We can see the signs of life over death in family experience. A young couple grieves at the death of their baby; a year or two later, a child is born. Not that any child can replace another; nevertheless, it is a fact that in the order of life and death, death and life, life affirms itself over death.

The Scriptures throw light on the meaning of our experience and we trust these two, always together, to guide us toward understanding. How then shall we understand our tears?

Our tears testify to the incompleteness of life as we experience it and they point with authority to its ultimate redemption and completion in Christ. We should not feel ashamed of our tears; they tell us a great truth. "Behold, the dwelling of God is with men. . . . He will wipe away every tear from their eyes, and death shall be no more."

My Prayer for This Day

Dear Father, I have not often thanked you for my tears, but I do now, because I begin to understand them. Help me to shed tears as Jesus did; he wept for others and not for himself. If I cannot help crying sometimes for myself, remind me that I am made complete through Jesus, whose death is the whole world's grief, and whose resurrection is the world's hope and mine. Through Jesus I ask this prayer. Amen.

The Blessing

Behold, I make all things new. . . . To the thirsty I will give water without price from the fountain of

the water of life. He who conquers shall have this
heritage, and I will be his God and he shall be my
son.

(Rev. 21:5–7)

EVENING

A Prayer for the Night

Lord God of all, I now entrust myself to you once
again. Let me rest in you, knowing that even in this
sorrow your great renewing work goes forward in
the world and in me. In Jesus' Name. Amen.

A Theme for Meditation

Behold, I make all things new.

(Rev. 21:5)

That is his promise!

When someone makes a promise, there is
nothing to analyze or argue. We simply await its
fulfillment. Time may pass; conditions must be
met, but if we trust the one who promises, we take
joy in living each day in the light of the promise.
We expect the good to happen.

God has made a promise: "He will wipe away
every tear . . . and death shall be no more." We
believe this and abide quietly and hopefully in it.
His intention is all-embracing: "Behold, I make all
things new."

As you reflect on all that occupies your mind, name aspects of your life that you would like to be made new. After each one, repeat the promises. Let your mind rest in them. Ask God to accomplish his renewing work in you.

DAY FOUR
Affliction

MORNING

Dedication of the Day

Lord God of hosts, may your Name be holy. Today let me behold you in your majesty and your mercy. Give me a special openness to your Spirit, so that in everything that happens and in the silences between happenings I may know that you are leading me. I dedicate this day to you. Give me light, I pray, in the Name of my Lord Jesus Christ. Amen.

Adoration

Thou, O Lord, art good and forgiving,
    abounding in steadfast love to all who call on thee.
Give ear, O Lord, to my prayer;
    hearken to my cry of supplication. . . .

Thou art great and doest wondrous things,
  thou alone art God.

(Ps. 86:5–6, 10)

A Word to Memorize

I will all the more gladly boast of my weaknesses,
that the power of Christ may rest upon me.

(2 Cor. 12:9)

Who really "boasts" of a squeaky voice, poor spelling, a moody disposition, or a physical handicap? No one. That is the force of St. Paul's statement: exactly because we have nothing to boast about in our weaknesses, Christ specially affirms himself there. To boast of our weaknesses is to boast in Christ and his gifts. Such "boasts" are confessions of our own dependence on Christ. To repeat today's verse is to boast not in ourselves, but to confess and praise Christ's strength in us.

"I will all the more gladly boast of my weaknesses, that the power of Christ may rest upon me."

The Blessing

May the God of peace himself sanctify you wholly; and may your spirit and soul and body be kept sound and blameless at the coming of our Lord Jesus Christ.

(1 Thess. 5:23)

NOON

A Prayer for the Hour

Lord, I thank you for every word you speak to me in the Scriptures, at worship in the congregation, or in conversation with believing friends. I thank you that where I am weak you are working in me to strengthen my body, nurture my spirit, and draw me closer to you. For what purpose am I here, O Lord? Take me for your own. In the Name of Jesus. Amen.

The Scriptures

Psalm 46. God present in the troubles of his people.
2 Cor. 12:1–10. St. Paul's "thorn in the flesh" a gift
of God.

A Reflection on Affliction

Everyone who must endure an unrelenting sorrow struggles to understand why. This is what is meant by affliction: grief that seems never to end, made all the more painful by the unanswered question of why it should be.

Certainly it would seem that affliction is an inhuman and wholly wrong form of suffering, yet faith sees it as an intrinsic part of the divine work in human life. Each person's life experience is different; and since God deals with all of us as we are, the meaning of affliction will differ from person to person.

St. Paul had some sort of physical problem, his "thorn in the flesh," which embarrassed and even handicapped him. God did not remove it, even though the apostle prayed earnestly for its cure. So St. Paul was obliged to understand it as part of God's will for him. He concluded that this problem was destined to remain with him for a good purpose: namely, to keep him from "becoming conceited" (NIV) by his extraordinary spiritual experiences and revelations.

The mystical experiences that St. Paul described in this letter did not so much humble him but tempted him to pride. How could he ever have come to understand this to be true—it was not the kind of truth anyone would enjoy facing—unless he had been confronted in some way? Furthermore, he had to recognize that his religious experiences were his alone. Since they were not shared with anyone, they could not have effective authority for others. So he made no claim on the basis of his personal experiences. But St. Paul knew that the experiences tempted him to consider himself superior, and that was where the "thorn" came in—to keep him humble. Such was the special meaning of his burden.

There is more than one way to respond to grief. Some seek imaginary relief through alcohol or other distractions. It is crucial to recognize that the divine grace is available so that suffering can be accepted and interpreted by faith, not denied and covered over. Affliction yields the discovery that God comes to us precisely when we are weakest. Furthermore, he comes continually. His grace is not quickly exhausted but is sufficient for the whole of life. With St. Paul, a believer who has discovered God's special concern through the experience of grief is truly blessed.

My Prayer for This Day

Dear Father, I confess that I often have difficulty with suffering. I commit myself to you and for a time I feel stronger, but then resentment creeps back and I am ashamed. Forgive me for my longing to escape. Help me to understand your unique work in me. Help me judge myself according to your great compassion for me. Through Jesus my Savior I pray. Amen.

The Blessing

Praise be to the God and Father of our Lord Jesus Christ, the all-merciful Father, the God whose consolation never fails us! He comforts us in all our troubles, so that we in turn may be able to comfort others in any trouble of theirs and to share with them the consolation we ourselves receive from God. . . . If you have part in the suffering, you have part also in the divine consolation.

(2 Cor. 1:3–7, NEB)

EVENING

A Prayer for the Night

Blessed Father, I commit myself to you now — for the night that comes, for the months that await me, and for eternity. Do not let affliction separate me from you. Whether I feel courageous or afraid, weak or strong, faithful or doubting, your love reaches out to me. Give me grace, for I would be faithful. In Jesus' Name. Amen.

A Theme for Meditation

In all these things we are more than conquerors through him who loved us.

(Rom. 8:37)

We — conquerors! How can that be? Only "through him who loved us." "Through him who loved us" is the theme for meditation tonight. *Everything* is through him who loved us: our birth, growth, adulthood, our very existence. This includes our pain. This is not to say that grief, disease, and death are in themselves good; it is to affirm that we experience them and respond to them in a special way — "through him who loved us." Much that happens to us in the course of a lifetime takes a lot of conquering. How are we ever to survive? "Through him who loved us."

So we are "more than conquerors" in all these

things. You know what is on your mind. Pull these troubling concerns into the open; name them and submit them to the authority of this blessed phrase: "More than conquerors through him who loved us." Let St. Paul's witness give you rest.

DAY FIVE
Death

MORNING

Dedication of the Day

Today, dear Lord, I propose to think about a subject that I dread. Can I dedicate this day to thinking about death? Yes, with your help. Give me a sense of your companionship, and send me your clarifying Spirit. In the Name of Jesus. Amen.

Adoration

To thee, O Lord, I lift up my soul.
O my God, in thee I trust,
    let me not be put to shame. . . .
Lead me in thy truth, and teach me,
    for thou art the God of my salvation;
    for thee I wait all the day long.

(Ps. 25:1–2, 5)

A Word to Memorize

Though I walk through the valley of the shadow of
  death, I fear no evil; for thou art with me.
                                        (Ps. 23:4)

The great psalm of comfort was written by a
poet who was quite willing to accept a shepherd's
care. To speak of himself under the metaphor of a
sheep was a truly humble decision. A sheep is
helpless; it has everything to fear. A central concern of this psalm is the fear that overwhelms the
defenseless when death lies in wait. But even in that
valley "I fear no evil; for thou art with me." The
shepherd is a trusted defender — he drives away the
threat with his rod.

"Though I walk through the valley of the
shadow of death, I fear no evil; for thou art with
me."

The Blessing

Turn thou to me, and be gracious to me;
  for I am lonely and afflicted.
Relieve the troubles of my heart,
  and bring me out of my distresses.
Consider my affliction and my trouble,
  and forgive all my sins.

                                    (Ps. 25:16–18)

NOON

A Prayer for the Hour

Blessed Lord, I thank you for your comfort. I am so defenseless. I am afraid of — I don't know what — and I am even more afraid that I might encounter something that will overwhelm me. Reassure me as I open your Word. Through Jesus my Lord. Amen.

The Scriptures

Psalm 23. God always with us.

Luke 22:39–45. Jesus' agony in the Garden of Gethsemane.

A Reflection on Death

All the pain that death causes is suffered by the living. From childhood we grow steadily in our awareness, until at length we discover — death. We have found the crisis of our very existence. How will we respond to an event that seems to put an end to everything we have valued, sought, created, loved, and protected?

Even persons with a well-established belief in God experience fear. Who believed in God more firmly than Jesus? Yet even he knew the terror of death. "Father, if thou art willing, remove this cup

from me." His suffering was enormous: "Being in
an agony he prayed more earnestly; and his sweat
became like great drops of blood falling down
upon the ground." The climax of his suffering came
the next day when in a moment of despair he felt
himself deserted by God. In the words of Psalm 22
he cried out, "My God, my God, why hast thou
forsaken me?"

Sensitive people feel a broad range of emotion at
the thought of death. It produces feelings of futil-
ity. Why fight it? How many operations, how
much more medicine is life worth? We are bound
to lose, no matter what we do.

While many older people feel that their lives are
complete, death comes to many, especially young
parents, as a vicious intruder, an enemy of children
in particular, something that does violence to the
right order of things.

How are we to respond to such feelings?

First, Christians are frank about death. Death is
not some little thing. It is the great denial of life and
all that life stands for. It is an enemy — the last
enemy to be destroyed, states St. Paul.

As universal as death is, Christians do not consider it part of the natural order. It is an enemy of
nature as God intends nature to be. Many people
today argue that death is part of life and we should
understand that it really belongs to nature. But
Christians do not make nature's happenings their

rule of what ought to be. God's completed nature, God's redeemed natural world, will be free of hostility, disease, anxiety, grief, and death.

Since death is the great enemy of Christians, they do not expect to be wholly free of fear. Fear can be relieved but it is inescapable. In our fear we turn to Christ. We ask him to send the Comforter he promised, the Holy Spirit, to go with us.

Christians do not surrender to death. We do not resign ourselves, if that means giving up, concluding that death really ends it all. Death is a valley through which we pass on our way to the City of God.

Christians praise God for having glorified himself in the raising of his Son to eternal life. Without death, that could not have been. Praise God for death? Not exactly! But he is its Master and reaches out to us through his own Son.

After praying to escape death, Jesus said: "Nevertheless not my will, but thine, be done." To say: "Not my will, but thine" is to invite God's own presence with us in the shadow of death. It is an act of faith through which we look beyond death to the perfect world that God intends and promises.

My Prayer for This Day

Dear Father, I want your will for my life. I ask that your glory might appear in my life and even in death, just as you glorified yourself in your Son's life and death. Help me to deal with death as he did; not without fear, perhaps, but in prayer and trust. "Thy will be done, on earth as it is in heaven." Amen.

The Blessing

Behold, I make all things new. . . . It is done! I am the Alpha and the Omega, the beginning and the end. To the thristy I will give water without price from the fountain of the water of life. . . . I will be his God and he shall be my son.

(Rev. 21:5–7)

EVENING

A Prayer for the Night

I have read your words of peace today, dear Lord. It comforts me that you walk ahead of me in this solemn valley. When the night came, you spoke to your Father; so I would speak to you and to him. I thank you that I am not alone. Amen.

A Theme for Meditation

Thou art the God of my salvation.

(Ps. 25:5)

It is necessary for us to know to whom we may turn when distressed. This is perfectly clear to the psalmist, to the evangelists who wrote the Gospels, and to all believers. We are encouraged and warmed by our friends; the doctors choose right medicines and treatment; but we say to the One whom we call Father: "Thou art the God of my salvation." It helps us maintain orientation to keep this phrase clearly before us. Bring your mind back to it and rest in it.

DAY SIX

Resurrection

MORNING

Dedication of the Day

On this day, O Lord, I remember your promise of life eternal. Let the day be blessed by your assurance; help my mind be attentive to your Word. I commit myself to you today in trust that you have come to me, that you do come to me, and that you will come again in your everlasting kingdom. Through Jesus my Lord I pray. Amen.

Adoration

Thou dost keep him in perfect peace,
   whose mind is stayed on thee,
   because he trusts in thee. . . .
   O Lord, we wait for thee;
thy memorial name
   is the desire of our soul.

My soul yearns for thee in the night,
    my spirit within me earnestly seeks thee.

                              (Isa. 26:3, 8–9)

A Word to Memorize

Thou dost keep him in perfect peace,
    whose mind is stayed on thee.

                              (Isa. 26:3)

In this passage in Isaiah, peace of mind and the promise of resurrection are brought together. The Hebrew people often suffered defeat. Their prophets taught them that such pain was a consequence of having forgotten their origin in God's great acts of creation and special calling. If they wanted peace and prosperity, they must fix their expectation on the God who had disclosed himself to their forebears.

Through the long desert experience, the difficulties of the conquest of the new land, and the political instability of the tribal period, a beloved king, David, finally unified the people. They worshiped God in his holy mountain, Zion. God had kept his promise. The time of fulfillment had come.

Then the Hebrew nation fell apart. Were the Hebrews confronting a broken promise, a divine failure? How could any believer know peace of mind in such conditions?

Isaiah offered an answer: God will re-create the nation. "The dead shall live, their bodies shall rise."

To entrust the nation, the church, the family, and oneself to God is to find peace.

"Thou dost keep him in perfect peace, whose mind is stayed on thee."

The Blessing

Trust in the Lord for ever,
    for the Lord God
    is an everlasting rock. . . .
O Lord, thou wilt ordain peace for us,
    thou has wrought for us all our works.

(Isa. 26:4, 12)

NOON

A Prayer for the Hour

Blessed Father, I have seen your work. I glorify your Name for coming to me in my need. Let me understand your promises; show me how they embrace all my concerns. Give me the light of your Spirit, in the Name of your Son Jesus. Amen.

The Scriptures

Isa. 26:16-19. The divine promise of the resurrection for the whole people and every person.
John 11:1-44. The story of the raising of Lazarus; basic teaching by Jesus about resurrection.

A Reflection on the Resurrection

To deny death in one way or another — by declaring it unreal, perhaps nothing but a form of sleep — is almost instinctive. Some religions seek to cope with our natural dread of death by renaming it or exalting it. The Bible is brutally realistic about death. No airy religion of flowers and sprites is taught here.

Jesus was quick to correct the disciples when they took his metaphor of sleep literally. "Jesus told them plainly, 'Lazarus is dead.' " Martha confirmed it: "Lord, by this time there will be an odor."

But Jesus had timed his visit with the intention of affirming another reality. "Did I not tell you that if you would believe you would see the glory of God?" He then prayed that what he was about to do would persuade the onlookers that God was true, and Lazarus came out of the grave on command. Once unmistakably dead, he now lived. The purpose of the miracle — and the reason the story is in the New Testament — was not so much to comfort Lazarus' family, which it did, as to affirm the authority of God in the world. So death itself was forced to serve God.

The miracle used the harsh reality of death to point to the truly conclusive reality of life. If death were a masquerade, a deception, or a natural thing easily accepted, resurrection itself would be unreal or meaningless. And without his act of overcoming death, God would not be disclosed in his glory.

The heart of the miracle lay not in the reconstitution of the flesh of Lazarus, for his flesh was still mortal. What was crucial was that the witnesses should see the glory of God. Mary, Martha, and Lazarus knew that glory firsthand. We share in it as we follow Jesus through death into life. Resurrection is more than restored flesh. It speaks to us of the fulfillment of the whole intention of God for the world, including ourselves.

My Prayer for This Day

Blessed Father, I pray not only for the healing of my grief but that I may see the glory of God. Give me hope in the resurrection, not just because I love the one I have lost but also because I have seen your glory. I thank you for every act by which you renew your scarred creation and heal our sorrow. Let me rest in your forgiveness and your healing. Through Jesus Christ my Lord. Amen.

The Blessing

I will not leave you desolate; I will come to you. Yet a little while, and the world will see me no more, but you will see me; because I live, you will live also.

(John 14:18–19)

EVENING

A Prayer for the Night

Blessed Lord, let the night be brilliant with the light of your presence. I am yours, happy or grieving, and I give myself to you afresh. Let the comfort you give teach me that you are with me in your glory. Grant me peace, rest, and healing in the Name of my Savior. Amen.

A Theme for Meditation

> Thou dost keep him in perfect peace,
>   whose mind is stayed on thee.
>
> (Isa. 26:3)

"Perfect peace!" Peace that is untroubled by the fear that it will end in war. Peace that knows no anxiety lest health degenerate into illness, life into death. To be "stayed on thee" is to fix the mind on the mighty acts of God through the whole Bible. Each of God's deeds confirms his promise and reaffirms his trustworthiness. He delivered the Hebrews from slavery, nourished them in the desert, led them into a land of their own, gave them a great king, sent prophets to teach and rebuke them, and finally sent his own Son. To ponder all this is to enter into God's peace.

Think about Jesus' command: "Lazarus, come forth" (KJV). He speaks to us. "Come forth—from fear, dullness, distraction, preoccupation, and affliction. Come forth into life that lasts and therefore gives peace." Repeat the memory verse and let it give you peace for the night.

DAY SEVEN
The Kingdom Life

MORNING

Dedication of the Day

Blessed Lord, you have spoken to me of eternal life, of faith and the kingdom that you have brought to the world. I am a child of this world. I long for your kingdom and for life under your Lordship. I dedicate myself to thinking upon your great works, your own Spirit, and the new world you have established among us. Help me believe. Through Jesus Christ. Amen.

Adoration

"Great indeed . . . is the mystery of our religion: He was manifested in the flesh, vindicated in the Spirit, seen by angels, preached among the nations, believed on in the world, taken up in glory." Blessed is the Name of the Lord. Amen.

(1 Tim. 3:16)

A Word to Memorize

Faith, hope, love abide, these three; but the greatest of these is love.

(1 Cor. 13:13)

If we could understand the whole meaning of love, we would always abide in the kingdom of God. "Thou shalt love the Lord thy God . . . ; and thy neighbor as thyself," said Jesus. "On these hang all the law and the prophets" (KJV). We need rules for practical reasons, but they need to be based on something that justifies them. In the Old Testament the divine righteousness was the foundation of the law. To this the New Testament adds love. If we were fully formed by love and if love had already driven out greed and consuming self-concern, we would not need rules. But as we are, we need rules to tell us clearly what love does and does not do. When the righteousness of God finally conquers us, rules will become unnecessary. Love wrote them, and mature love knows them instinctively.

To live in love is to live in the divine kingdom. "Faith, hope, love abide, these three; but the greatest of these is love."

The Blessing

The love of Christ controls us, because we are convinced that one has died for all; therefore all have died. And he died for all, that those who live might live no longer for themselves but for him who for their sake died and was raised.

(2 Cor. 5:14–15)

NOON

A Prayer for the Hour

Blessed Father, Lord and King, it is not easy for me to grasp the kingdom life. Love I know, but in forms that are lower by far than your love. I do not even love myself very well. Grant me a higher vision of love and a truer sense of your kingdom within me. Through Jesus our Lord. Amen.

The Scriptures

Psalm 91. The security of divine love.
1 Corinthians 13. St. Paul's great love lyric.

A Reflection on the Kingdom Life

"Love" is at once the most abused word in the English language and the most richly furnished with unrealized meaning. When a man declares his love for a young woman, what can he know of the tests and proofs of love that await him? Human beings experience love a piece at a time, so to speak: as children we know love that is dependent on parents; then romantic love, sexual love, and love of children; and eventually the love that affirms itself in serving another, including sexual self-denial.

To St. Paul, love is ultimate. It never fails, even though great gifts and talents may vanish. Love survives the body through which we ordinarily express it. Love is the name of the force that holds everything together. Love is of God; indeed, God is love.

God translated from an idea into a style of daily living — that is love. To be in Christ is to exist in love, our lives flowing forth from God just as Jesus was constantly sustained by his Father. We glimpse an analogy of this love in romantic feelings: being in love, as we say. Everything is suffused with a lovely quality — even the sparrows seem to sing our song of joy. The kingdom life involves an outreaching, joyous concern for the world such as the youth in love feels for everything in sight. The difference is that life in the kingdom is not a matter of maintaining a mood of excitement. Rather, it is to exist in the light of Christ's revolutionary death and resurrection, to be seized by the stunning realization that he is among us, rich in love, power, and light. When the Christian reaches out to the world, it is Christ's own outreaching love and concern rather than a grasping demand on the world.

Those who have passed through a valley of grief, even the approach of death itself, and who have known the protection, love, and companionship of the Great Shepherd, understand the "kingdom life."

Some speak of "mountaintop experiences," such as St. Paul's heavenly visions (2 Cor. 12:1-4). But it is in the valleys where we come to know that Christ is our shepherd. Whether we live or die, we emerge into a new world of his care, his Lordship, his kingdom.

My Prayer for This Day

Blessed Father in heaven, I long to know your kingdom more fully. I have glimpsed it in your Word — but my life is incomplete. Help me commit myself freshly to life in the light of the cross and the resurrection. Grant me your Spirit, and fill me with the joy of your kingdom. In the Name of Christ our Lord. Amen.

The Blessing

Our soul waits for the Lord;
    he is our help and shield.
Yea, our heart is glad in him,
    because we trust in his holy name.
Let thy steadfast love, O Lord, be upon us,
    even as we hope in thee.

(Ps. 33:20-22)

EVENING

A Prayer for the Night

Blessed God, you are the king of the night as well as of the day; king of the realms we fear as well as the realms of joy. Make this night your own, and take possession of me as one who dwells in it securely. Whether I am lonely or serene, joyous or grieving, come to me as my shepherd and comfort me. I would love you as you have long loved me. Amen.

A Theme for Meditation

Love never ends.

(1 Cor. 13:8)

As God knows no "end," love never ends. God's kingdom is a kingdom of love; since God's kingdom knows no end, "love never ends."

Meditate tonight on the boundlessness of the divine love, on Christ's holy invitation to join him in an eternal life of love. Let your mind be captured by the thought. To be his captive is to enter his kingdom! You may repeat the Lord's Prayer.